Sp

SPEAKING OF FRIENDSHIP

Warm and Witty Comments By Well-Known Personalities

Selected by
Julie Clardy and Kathleen Saving

Illustrated by Lilian Weytjens

HALLMARK EDITIONS

INTRODUCTION

Friendship seems in some ways to be the poor relative of Love. Love commands the rapt attention of the poets and songwriters, the novelists and playwrights. But what about Friendship?

Compared to Love, Friendship seems to be lacking something. In fact, it's just the opposite. Friendship holds a constancy, a trust and an unselfish spirit that Love may fail to attain.

Most of us are blessed with at least one Friendship that lasts a very long time, perhaps a lifetime. We are so sure of it, we hardly think of it at all. But there it is, smoothing out the rough places, laughing, sharing memories and special secrets, turning nothing days into good times, turning happiness into a celebration of life.

Speaking of Friendship may seem a little like speaking of breathing, of your own heartbeat, of sunrise, sunset. But speak of it we will! For in these pages are some very special, very personal thoughts about friendship written for this book by well-known personalities from many fields.

As we read their words, hopefully we may pause and look around to see, as if for the first time, someone very dear to us who has been there all along.   Dean Walley

It is said that most friendships are formed by chance, from proximity or necessity. But is that so evil? All it means is that in any circumstances of living, friends will sort themselves out from the mass of human encounters. It shows that friendship is based upon character more than any other one thing. It can transcend all surface differences of age, sex, wealth, race, class, education, experience, but character, never. Its other chief component is mutuality. Unrequited love can go on for years, but one-sided friendship simply dissolves, or rather, it never comes into being. By definition, friendship is reciprocal, yet it holds this element of selfishness: the more completely one becomes oneself, the more soundly based his friendships will be.

My definition of friendship? Simply this: When the House Un-American Activities Committee asks you to rat on your friends, you don't do it.

Friendship involves the total concern and compassion for another fellow human being "in times of peace and in times of war."

It encompasses

- F ondness
- R eliance
- I ntensity
- E steem
- N eighborliness
- D evotedness
- S incerity
- H armony
- I nterest
- P atience

These ten virtues comprise the depths of *true* friendship—love of one human being for another!

I went out in the daffodil moonlight of Mid-May to see whether the birds had eaten all of the hamburger rolls I tossed at the bottom of the steps to the beach. The birds drowsed in hidden nests but there sat a racoon on the lowest step, holding a roll in both hands. Lifting his dark triangular face, he stared at me with onyx eyes.

"Welcome," I said softly, "I am happy to see you. Sharing is a pleasure."

He knew, strangely, that I was a friend. All the hunting, trapping, killing between his kind and mine was forgotten. We visited, both of us less lonely for a time.

Afterward I thought about friendship and what it means. It means, I thought, a giving of ourselves and a taking of warmth from another. It is a priceless gift which we all have to give.

It never means saying, "I am going to tell you something for your own good." Or, "You made a bad mistake and I feel it is my duty to say so."

It means saying, "Thank you for being you. I want you to know just thinking of you warms my heart. May we walk hand in hand through both sunny hours and sorrowful times."

friendship is holding each other
as you are
until you both become what you can become
helped on by the power of that holding love

DR. BILLY GRAHAM

I think it is appropriate that the great old hymn "What a Friend We Have in Jesus" so elevates the earthly bond of friendship. For in our friends we find the truth, the strength and the unwavering faith that are very close to the Kingdom of Heaven. Thank God for my friends. They have stood by me through the years, sharing both my joy and my sorrow, enriching my life, reaching out to me wherever I might be. And Thank God my friends in Christ will be with me always as we travel beyond this life into Life Everlasting. Friends are like the hands of God reaching out to us here on earth — strong hands that clasp our own and draw us ever closer to our Father in Heaven.

After much deliberation, I don't really know if I can define Friendship. I do know that it is the most valuable gift one can give or receive. It knows neither time nor space. In Friendship there is no death—only Life. In true Friendship, one doesn't really care whether they are the giver or the receiver and above all— Friendship means LOVE and LOVE means Friendship.

MAMIE D. EISENHOWER

The friendship of our many friends has meant a great deal to me all through the years and still does. Friends have played a great part in our lives for which I am grateful.

The spontaneous art
   In friendship casting
Is to give of heart
   Without anyone asking.

Good friendship comes
   From one least able,
In a sharing of crumbs
   Off his barren table.

JOYCE CAROL OATES

He said: "When I went to turn on the gas
I saw the stove was an electric stove—
How could I kill myself
    with an electric stove?"

So he ran outside to the streets
    of Detroit
to see what noises might dilute his pain.

And now
it is a decade later and he
    has survived to retell
that hour as an anecdote
    we have heard before.
The two of us smile in chorus
    at our friend.
We do not quite acknowledge
    the terror of that hour
and he does not acknowledge it, now,
having lived to speak of it.

Our voices skim over terror as over
a difficult passage of music
notes barbed and jangling and poisonous
on our warm tongues.

There is a forbidden zone between friends
which no one enters: it is wired
    too tensely.
There, a breath might expand into a scream.
No, we will not acknowledge
    the pain of his joke,
no, not the possibility, not death,
    not the death of friends.
It is not friendly.
We will not give permission
    to one another to die:
it is not a friendly conversation.

ED SULLIVAN

To have friends, *you* must be a friend.

HENRY DREYFUSS

On the instant of meeting
After a long separation
And with no sense of a time lapse,
To rediscover an easy
    and comfortable relationship—
This is one of the joys of friendship.

ERMA BOMBECK

A friend does not go on a diet
when you are fat.

A friend does not show you the extravagant
flowers she received for Mother's Day
when you received a plastic elephant
pencil sharpener.

A friend does not find humor in a
mother-in-law who wore a black armband
to your wedding.

A friend does not clean house until
her children are grown and you can
do it together.

A friend is just a plain, wonderful person...
like yourself.

DR. DAVID GOODMAN

People need people. Period! And older people particularly need some companionship to get over the gray times in their lives.

Yet older people tend to withdraw within themselves, longing for company yet lacking that bit of extra energy needed to go out and get it. What they must do is to shake out of their lethargy and give friendship a chance. It's no great risk. Everybody wants a friend. Everybody is willing to be a friend once the warm hand of welcome is extended to them.

Friends are particularly important with our new longevity. We now live to be seventy, eighty, even ninety. The children are grown and gone. A long dreary prospect of lonely days lies before us unless we manage to bring old friends back into our lives, as well as make new ones.

It was America's great psychologist-philosopher William James who said that over our moods we have no control. They come willy nilly, the sad ones often staying a long while. But our actions are under the direction of the will. We can will to act.

We can will to make contact with our old friends; we can will to meet and greet new acquaintances with that ready smile, that cheery word that turns them into friends.

Why don't we?

The main reason is that with the sensitiveness that comes with the advancing years, we are afraid to get rebuffed, to get hurt.

But the other one is afraid, too. It's a question of who will smile first. Take the risk to be the warmhearted one and you break the curse of loneliness. The other will smile, too. Then there he (she) is, your new friend!

This way you will in time have several new friends to add to your old ones. Life will be warm and cozy again. Also interesting, which is important! As long as we are interested in life, we stay alive and well. Friendship is the healing balm of our golden years.

Friendship may end in love, but love never ends in friendship.

JOHN V. LINDSAY

Friendship is those Republicans who still speak to you after you become a Democrat.

I went away to visit the place at which I put in by far the greater part of my grown-up life, and where I had so many good friends. But it appears rather forcibly now that I've come to that time of life marked by the loss of friends: divorce, illness, death, retirement, moving away... down to the lesser extreme of a certain withdrawal from society, all these have been working away at the fabric of a community, and already I had to view myself as a time-traveler, maybe some minor sort of Rip Van Winkle, awakening at home among strangers. Space-traveler, as well, for until the advent of jet airplanes one could not make the journey out and back so often, nor with such insouciance. Friendship has been a most sustaining thing to me—but there is this other end to the matter, where either we desert or they do, the friends; of whom the poet Donald Justice so beautifully and elegiacally says, "Come, Memory, let us seek them among the shades."

BOB COUSY

We often hear the cliché that you can count your friends on one hand and even this may be an exaggeration. I think that possibly the two most scarce commodities to find in our contemporary society are sincerity and genuine friends. Obviously similar to a romantic relationship, friendship is based on an unselfish, sacrificing attitude towards the partner involved, in which case both parties discover that true friendship is one of the most satisfying and gratifying relationships in life.

MARGARET CHASE SMITH

Friendship is measured more in terms of silent acts than in terms of effusive words...in understanding of differences...and in times of difficulties.

Of all our relationships friendship is the least easily defined, the most subject to change and therefore the most fragile. We are, as sociologists never tire of telling us, a very mobile people. We change our addresses — even our classes — a lot. And friendships perish in the process — without our wanting or meaning them to. I spend quite a few of my idle moments now wondering what ever became of people with whom once, ten or twenty years ago, I shared my most intimate thoughts and feelings, and who shared theirs with me, and to whom I no longer know how to get a Christmas card. Even so, I feel that if I chanced to run into them on the street I could probably pick up our conversation pretty much where we left it. For the point is not whether they know exactly how many children I have or how, precisely, I spend my days, but that once, for some reason, we were able to entrust to one another's safe keeping a secret, sacred part of ourselves — loves and hates, hopes and fears that would otherwise have gone unspoken, but which we needed to bring out in the light and examine with someone else. I've left so many bits and pieces of myself with so many whom I would probably have difficulty recognizing now. I am the repository of so many fragments of others who would pass me on the street unseeing. We no longer need each other; new friends fill the old, endless need for intimacy. But the need we shared in the long ago binds us together with the invisible ties of shared memory, which is one definition of the word history, which, in turn, is one of the great forces that civilizes and humanizes us. My point is that we should not mourn the decay of old friendships, but try to keep alive the memory of what was good in them so that we may also keep alive the will and skill to make new ones — so that we can keep the chain of history — even if it is only personal history — growing, linking us to new times and places as strongly as we are anchored to the old ones.

A state of serene trust, totally happy making, inspired not through the competition of emotions but through unquestioning, simple faith.

FLORENCE B. JACOBS

We were discussing it
a week ago,
how loosely it is used to signify
acquaintances or people passing by
and meaning little; how few really know
the depth of meaning in the countersign
we signal with so freely,
    "friend of mine."

There are a hundred vivid similes;
a fuller rapture when our joy is high;
when life is chill, a flame
    to warm us by;
in utter pain, remembered ecstasies....
Oh, words are weak! But you
    to whom I write
know what it is, alive
and rich and bright!

For once or twice within a lifetime, we
find someone whom we love
    for that which is
dependent not on looks or qualities...
call it soul, spirit, personality...
the thing which is no other but that one,
the thing which will not die
    when life is done.

And that we join to us in such a way
that neither fate nor change
    nor ill repute
can ever grow so strong as to refute
the bond, nor time bring any least decay....
Friendship like this, if life
    holds only one
it is well lived and heaven half begun.

MARLIN PERKINS

All of the love, trust and companionship that friendship represents to each of us can never be more fully realized than when such a deep relationship develops between a human being and an animal.

Whether it is a boy and his dog, a man and his horse, an invalid with a devoted house cat or some very special people like Joy and George Adamson, whose friendship with a lioness called Elsa became a legend in our time, those fortunate enough to experience and share such a trustful relationship with an animal will cherish this forever along with all the other blessings of being alive.

It is friendship in its purest form. Unquestioning, uncritical, loyal and asking nothing from us but our friendship in return.

HENRY WOLF

Someone who sits on a plane next to you
and makes you less afraid of crashing.

Someone who recommends a movie to see
and you know that you'll like it.

Someone who calls you for no reason at all.

Someone you haven't seen in three years
and with whom you are back to where
you left off within three minutes.

Someone who is not afraid
to act foolish when you are there.

Someone who will tell you a story
about himself in which he comes out badly.

Someone who'll laugh at your joke
at a party even though it's the third time
he's heard it.

Someone you'd buy gifts for that you'd
love to own yourself.

Someone who remembers your birthday
long after you have stopped
being useful to him.

Someone you like because you like
yourself better in his company.

Friendship, like Gaul, is divided into three parts:

    Superficial, temporary friendship

    Average, casual friendship

    Warm, deep, lasting friendship

Everyone of us during our lifetime experiences all three kinds of friendship, but the fortunate person is the one who has a preponderance of really true friendships.

I work in motion pictures as a costume designer, and many of my friends are in category No. 2 because actors, actresses, directors and producers, all the personnel of a studio, come and go, but even then among the casual group you occasionally find a really lasting friendship. I am very fortunate to have all three kinds of friendship (with a preponderance of friendship No. 3).

GLORIA VANDERBILT

Friendship is a commitment. A trust. It consists of not letting that person down when they need you. It is rare and should be treasured.

There is an old cliché which is no less viable because it's a chestnut, which says, "A friend is one who knows all about you and loves you just the same."

All of us have faults — some of which we try to conceal and correct, others that are apparent — and it seems to me, today, we need a great deal of tolerance and understanding.

Understanding of other people's problems, faults and differences of opinion.

When we have been able to achieve that kind of objectivity, it seems to me, we have learned to understand the true meaning of friendship.

BISHOP FULTON J. SHEEN

Friendship is wanting to be needed—

Life is like a great ship with room aboard for many people. Friends who hop on and off, charming but quickly forgotten. Friends who sail along when all is placid, adding pleasure to the trip. And those friends whom you can depend on, fair weather or foul; who will ride out the very worst storms with you and see you safely to port. I love this spacious and sturdy vessel and christened it long ago: My ship of friends. The *Friendship.*

There are ways in which friendship can be even more rewarding than love. It lacks the often rending intensity of love, but because of that it may have more enduring stability. You may fall in love several times, but old friendship can survive every time. Friends lack the total intimacy of love, but the close handclasp of proven friendship is like the fingers kissing.

Immediately, this little sentiment came to mind: "A friend is one who knows all about you—but loves you just the same."

HARRIET NELSON

Friendship is a very special, very precious commodity. It has some of the elements of *loving* and some of the elements of *liking*. A friend is someone you can turn to in times of trouble. A friend is someone whose company you enjoy. There are many degrees of friendship—from casual to intimate.

I have a picture in my photograph album that I treasure. It was taken in Des Moines, Iowa, when I was four years old. Standing alongside of me is another little girl. She was five. We are holding hands. She lived next door and she was my friend.

When I was seventeen, I toured in vaudeville on the Keith Circuit with a musical company called "The Harry Carroll Revue." There were four other teenage girls in the troop and we became close friends. We still visit or talk on the telephone together at least once a week. We call ourselves the *Chums*. A chum is a very warm, very close friend.

I also have boyfriends—three of them. They are people I like very much and love very much. I guess you would call them very, *very* special friends. Their names are Ozzie, David and Ricky.

ANNE SEXTON

A friend is someone who listens to your dreams the next morning. A friend is someone who bails you out when you're arrested. A friend is someone who brings horseradish and littleneck clams to your deathbed.

CHET HUNTLEY

Implicit in the bond of friendship is the understanding that whatever befalls you is important
to me—but we need never say so.

DORIS CHALMA BROCK

Friendship is a miraculous happening between people...a warm, glowing, intangible understanding that reaches from one to another. Friendship is independent of logic and refuses to be categorized...it is unique, inexpressibly dear and to be cherished. It is a gift freely given.

BARBARA WALTERS

Friendship is the purest form of affection.

EVAN CONNELL

Somebody told an unpleasant story about one of my friends; I didn't believe the story, and I said so. It might have been true, but that was irrelevant.

THE CONTRIBUTORS

ERMA BOMBECK

The writer of a syndicated column, "At Wit's End," Ms. Bombeck has authored several books based on her column including "*Just Wait Till You Have Children of Your Own.*"

DORIS CHALMA BROCK

Iowa free-lancer Doris Chalma Brock has drawn heavily upon her own homemaking and nursing experience in her poetry.

SHIRLEY CHISHOLM

The first Black congresswoman, Shirley Chisholm, has written the story of her 1972 presidential campaign, entitled *The Good Fight.*

EVAN CONNELL

Mr. Bridge and *Mrs. Bridge* are two of the most popular novels by Evan Connell, former editor of *Contact* magazine and recipient of the Rockefeller Foundation Grant.

BOB COUSY

After his successful career with the Boston Celtics, basketball's "Little Big Man," Bob Cousy, turned to coaching.

BING CROSBY

Crooner and actor Bing Crosby is also known for hosting the Bing Crosby National Pro-Am Golf Tournament.

HENRY DREYFUSS

Industrial designer, inventor and corporate consultant Henry Dreyfuss served as a member of the Board of Directors of Ford Foundation and authored a book of international signs.

MICHAEL DRURY
As an author of books of poetry, short stories and magazine articles, Ms. Drury has displayed an uncommon perception and understanding of life.

MAMIE D. EISENHOWER
Many honors have been bestowed upon former First Lady Mamie Eisenhower for her untiring service to this country.

PAUL ENGLE
A distinguished poet, Paul Engle's works also include *Golden Child*, a story about the true meaning of Christmas.

DR. DAVID GOODMAN
A strong belief in marriage has been evidenced in the writings of Dr. David Goodman, marriage counselor and humanitarian.

DR. BILLY GRAHAM
In 1949, evangelist Billy Graham began his nationwide crusades, which later became worldwide.

EDITH HEAD
Fashion designer Edith Head has received numerous Academy Awards for her movie costumes.

FLORENCE HENDERSON
A star of television's "The Brady Bunch," Florence Henderson began her career as a Broadway singer.

MARJORIE HOLMES
The author of *Two from Galilee*, Ms. Holmes began her writing career with a newspaper column, "Love and Laughter," and has authored many books.

CHET HUNTLEY
Virtually every major award for radio-television journalism has been bestowed upon national news broadcaster Chet Huntley.

FLORENCE B. JACOBS
Popular Maine poet and essayist Florence Jacobs has contributed poetry and prose to many national magazines and was elected to the Poetry Society of America in 1960.

CORITA KENT
The bold, graphic artwork of Corita Kent, former nun and professor of art at Immaculate Heart College, has become famous throughout the world.

ANN LANDERS
As a nationally syndicated advice columnist for many years, Ms. Landers has written numerous books and has been active in humanitarian causes.

JOHN V. LINDSAY
After being elected mayor of New York City in 1965 as a Republican, Mr. Lindsay switched parties in 1971.

ART LINKLETTER
The nation's master of merriment, Art Linkletter, both wrote and hosted the "People Are Funny" and "House Party" television shows.

HARRIET NELSON
The matriarch of the famous Nelson family, Harriet, along with Ozzie, returned in the fall of 1973 with a new television series called "Ozzie's Girls."

HOWARD NEMEROV
The book *Gnomes and Occasions* represents some of educator, author, critic and poet Howard Nemerov's best work.

JOYCE CAROL OATES
A brilliant poet and short-story writer, Ms. Oates's recent books include *Marriages and Infidelities* and *Angel Fire.*

PATTI PAGE
One of the top female vocalists of all times, Ms. Page's most famous recording, "Tennessee Waltz," was the number one song of 1951.

MARLIN PERKINS
As the originator and host of television's "Zoo Parade" and "Wild Kingdom," Marlin Perkins has worked closely with animals for many years.

TONY RANDALL
An actor for many years, Tony Randall recreated the role of perfectionist Felix Unger in the television series "The Odd Couple."

RICHARD SCHICKEL
As a free-lance writer and film critic for *Life* magazine, Mr. Schickel has commented expertly about the world of the cinema.

ANNE SEXTON
College students throughout the United States have enjoyed the recitations of Pulitzer Prize winning poet Anne Sexton.

BISHOP FULTON J. SHEEN
As an educator and writer, Bishop Sheen has contributed widely to radio, television and the religious press.

MARGARET CHASE SMITH
After serving as a congresswoman, Margaret Chase Smith was elected to the United States Senate from Maine in 1948.

ED SULLIVAN
Television's foremost emcee, Ed Sullivan, has introduced America to new acts and entertainers from all over the world.

GLADYS TABER

A columnist for *Ladies' Home Journal* for nineteen years, Gladys Taber has written numerous books about life at Stillmeadow Farm.

GLORIA VANDERBILT

Actress and artist Gloria Vanderbilt has exchanged the Broadway stage for one-man art shows in New York.

DIANA VREELAND

The former fashion editor of *Harper's Bazaar*, Ms. Vreeland rose to editor-in-chief of *Vogue*.

BARBARA WALTERS

A television news reporter, Ms. Walters joined the news team of the "Today" show in 1961.

HENRY WOLF

As art director for several magazines and executive of Trahey-Wolf Advertising, Inc., Henry Wolf has helped to shape the face of the modern magazine.

Set in Intertype Walbaum, a light,
open typeface designed by
Justus Erich Walbaum (1768-1839),
who was a typefounder at Weimar.
Printed on Hallmark Eggshell Book paper.
Designed by Lilian Weytjens.